Contents

Some words are shown in bold, **like this**.
You can find them in the glossary on page 22.

What is the internet?

The internet is a network of computers. It connects people using underground cables that stretch around the world.

We connect to the internet using our
tablets, smart phones and laptops.
The internet is a great place to learn,
have fun and keep in touch with friends.

How do people connect online?

People often use the internet to visit websites and learn new things. Many also **communicate** with each other using email and **social media**.

You can also play games with other people online. When you are connected to the internet you are "online".

Is being online fun?

Being online is like going on an adventure. It is fun and exciting.

However, you have to be prepared.
Just as on a real adventure, you don't
know who or what you will discover.

Who can help with the internet?

When you begin using the internet, ask a **trusted adult** to help you. She or he can set up your computer's security settings and online **passwords**.

She or he can also help you create a **screen name**. A screen name is a made-up name a person uses on some **social media** websites.

Is social media safe?

Social media is like an online club where you can chat with friends. However, you have to be careful about chatting with people you don't know.

Sometimes people pretend to be a friend when they want something from you.

Should I share my personal information?

It's important to keep any personal information off the internet. If a friend asks for your address or phone number, share that privately, on the phone or by email.

You should only use your full name or share photos with people you have met in person. Ask an adult to help you with privacy settings on **social media** sites.

Should I ever ignore emails?

Email is a great way to keep in touch with friends and family. It's important not to open emails from strangers.

Sometimes these emails contain **attachments** called viruses. They can harm your computer. It's best to delete such emails or ask an adult to help decide whether to open them.

What are cyberbullies?

Cyberbullies are people who say nasty things. They also spread lies about others online.

It's important never to reply to a cyberbully. You should never spread their messages. Instead, show their messages to a **trusted adult** for help.

How can I be a good digital citizen?

Being a good digital citizen means being polite online and respecting others. Remember to always report anything you think is harmful.

That will help make the internet an exciting, fun and safe adventure for everyone.

Glossary

 **attachment** file, such as a photo, that is sent as part of an email

 **communicate** to share information, thoughts or feelings

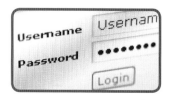 **password** secret code usually made up of a combination of letters, words or numbers

 **screen name** made-up name that a person uses when he or she are online

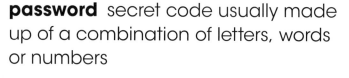 **social media** form of online communication where users create online communities to share information, ideas, messages, etc.

 **trusted adult** grown-up that you know well, who is honest and reliable

Find out more

Books

Digital Technology (Technology Timelines), Tom Jackson (Franklin Watts, 2016)

Our Digital World (Kids Get Coding), Heather Lyons (Wayland, 2016)

Understanding Computer Search and Research (Understanding Computing), Paul Mason (Raintree, 2016)

Websites

www.bbc.co.uk/education/subjects/zyhbwmn
This BBC website is designed to teach young learners about computers.

www.easyscienceforkids.com/all-about-computers/
This Easy Science For Kids website explains computers and their history.

www.factmonster.com/ipka/A0772279.html
This Factmonster website provides information and games about computers, technology and the internet for kids.

Index